# THE PRE-SCHOOL CRAFT BOOK

# THE PRE-SCHOOL CRAFT BOOK

## Activities for the 2 to 5's in kindergartens, groups, nursery schools, and at home

## TOY MARTIN

Illustrated by Ester Kasepuu

NC Press Limited
Toronto, 1985

Second Canadian Edition 1985

First published in Canada 1984 by
N C Press Limited
31 Portland Street
Toronto, Ontario,
CANADA M5V 2V9

Originally published in Australia 1981 by
A H & A W REED PTY LTD
2 Aquatic Drive Frenchs Forest NSW 2086

© Toy Martin 1981

Canadian Cataloguing-in-Publication Data
Martin, Toy.
 The pre-school craft book
 ISBN 0-920053-24-6
 1. Handicraft. 2. Education, Preschool. I. Title.
TT160.M37 1984  745.5  C84-098268-2

*Printed and bound in Canada by Hignell Printing*

# CONTENTS

# ABOUT THIS BOOK

Here are 83 craft projects for young children. Although the book is primarily aimed at pre-school use, the projects can certainly be done at home too. They are ideal for that special one-to-one time with your child.

The materials required for most of the activities are very basic. You can even pick a project by looking around the house and then at the materials list at the back of the book. You'll find that even if you've only got paper, scissors, stapler and tape on hand, there are still ten craft projects you can do straight away.

Pre-school craft should not just mean a general collage or open slather on the craft box (although both of these are great fun, every once in a while). It's just too boring, week after week—the child (and the parent where he or she is involved) will lose interest.

Some children will be able to do a project unaided—fine, let them. But don't reject a craft idea if a child can't handle it alone. In a group or at home, this is the time set aside from a busy week to do things *with* your child. Use it to the fullest. You cut, the child folds; you apply the paste, the child sticks the pieces down; you position the stapler, the child pushes; you hold the string taut, the child cuts with the scissors (two-handed grips allowed!). Craft time can be real quality time for all involved.

These craft projects were selected with several things in mind.

*The materials are usually fairly basic.* While the pre-school teacher may have a cupboard full of plastic bottles, wood shavings and shredded computer paper, most groups and homes do not. So the more easily accessible the materials, the better.

*The preparation time should not be great.* The craft organiser should not have to spend too much time mixing, cutting and so forth. The preparation can be flexible, depending on the ages of the children—i.e. for very young children, have pre-cut pieces; older ones can cut their own.

*Children want an immediate result.* They literally can't wait for the paint to dry or for the paper mâché to set. Projects using these materials are really for older school age children who have developed a bit of patience.

*The project can be a cheap, disposable toy—and hand made too!* It can be something to play with when craft time is over for the day. And when the toy breaks, you can just make another one.

*Many of the projects have an element of delight.* Making the Tiger Claws is interesting. But roaring and snarling and hissing—that's fun. And that's what the Tiger Claws project is all about!

The presentation of the craft project can be very important to youngsters. If the craft table is long or large, have two or three finished products on display. Set out the required materials so that each child can reach the paste, paper, staplers and so on from where she or he sits. If young children have to get up and walk to the paste, they're just as liable to be distracted and walk out the door to the sandpit! Try to set aside a display area for finished projects. That way, children can go on to paints, playdough, blocks or puzzles and yet still be able to find their craft project to take home. The project does not accidentally get squashed or lost in the meantime.

Listed under the materials section of many of the craft projects is the phrase 'materials for decorating'. These can be crayons (fat ones), felt tips (nice vivid colours, but only if you dare!), coloured paper and paste, and gummed coloured paper (that you just lick to stick on). Coloured chalk and coloured pencils are OK for decorating, but the chalk does smear easily and neither has the bright impact of colour that children seem to go for. Naturally, if you have plenty of storage space, many adds and ends can be added to the Materials-for-Decorating box. Tinfoil, scraps of material, yarn, buttons, cupcake papers all come in handy when it comes to the finishing touches on a craft project.

Below are some suggestions for a well-stocked craft box which doesn't take up too much room and is easily carried about.

| | |
|---|---|
| safety scissors | crayons |
| paste | string |
| small staplers | pipe cleaners |
| cello tape | plain white paper |
| double sided tape | |

There is one item that no craft box should be without — a great big bundle of genuine interest. If you've a good supply of that, your craft project will be successful — no matter what it looks like!

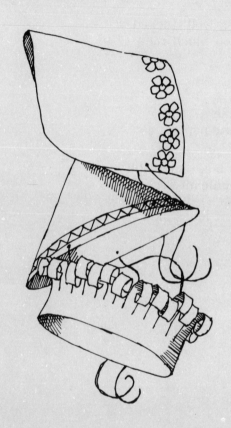

## Project 1

### Dutch Hat

paper, scissors, stapler, string, materials for decorating

Cut out a rectangle of paper about 30 cm × 25 cm. As shown in the illustration, take top corner A and top corner B, overlap and staple. Add string to tie under the chin, and decorate.

## Project 2

### Sun Hat

paper plate or circle of paper, scissors, stapler, string, materials for decorating

Cut away a quarter of the paper plate. Overlap the two cut edges and staple. Add string to tie under the chin, and decorate.

## Project 3

### Paper Crown

paper, scissors, stapler, pencil, materials for decorating

Cut paper into strips about 35 cm × 10 cm. Cut a fringe into one long edge of the paper, making sure that each piece of fringe is about 3 or 4 cm wide. After the fringe has been cut, roll up sections of the fringe around a pencil. When you take the pencil out, the fringe will remain curly. Decorate the crown. Check the child's head measurement and staple the crown accordingly.

11

Project 4

# Skull Cap

paper, stapler, scissors, cotton ball, paste, materials for decorating

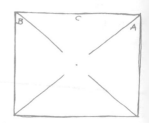

Cut the paper so it measures 30 cm × 25 cm. Mark the centre of the paper with a dot. From each of the four corners, cut towards the centre dot, but stop cutting about 5 cm from the centre. Pull A and B corners to overlap. Pull up C to meet A and B and put a staple at C. Do the same at the other end of the hat. Fold up the points of the hat if you want a sportier look! Paste a cotton ball pom pom on top and decorate the hat.

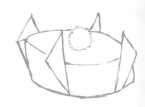

Project 5

# Indian Headband, Arm and Ankle Bands

heavy paper or lightweight cardboard, scissors, paste, coloured paper, stapler, string, pipe cleaner

Cut cardboard into strips about 4 cm wide and long enough to do the job. Paste on pieces of coloured paper for decorations. The headband can be stapled to fit, while the arm and ankle bands will all have to be fitted with two pieces of string. You can add Indian feathers by cutting out a narrow, oval shape and pasting or stapling a pipe cleaner down the centre. Leave a bit of the pipe cleaner extending so you can attach it to the headband. Make many parallel cuts into the edges of the oval shape. Near the back of the headband, make two small holes and attach the pipe cleaner through these.

# Project 6

white paper or newspaper, coloured paper, string, scissors, tape, materials for decorating

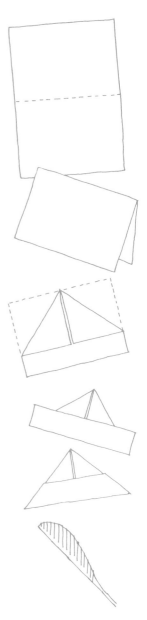

Begin with a piece of paper about 60 cm × 42 cm (a double page from a newspaper). Fold in half. Fold the two upper edges down to meet in the centre. Turn lower edges up to form the brim. Fold the points in and secure with tape so the hat does not come apart on the first wearing. Take a piece of coloured paper about 25 cm long and 7 cm wide. Fold it lengthwise and cut out a feather shape. Make a lot of parallel cuts to fringe the double edges. Without unfolding the paper, insert the plume and tape it in position. Cut two pieces of string for the chin strap. Decorate the hat.

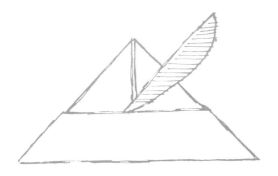

# PUPPETS

Project 7

# Dog on a Stick

paper, scissors, paddle pop stick, tape, materials for decorating

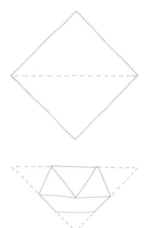

Cut the paper into a 15 cm square. Fold the square into a triangle. Take the left hand corner of the long edge and bring it down so that the point touches the middle of the dog's face. Do the same with the right hand corner. Fold the bottom point of the original triangle back to form the dog's chin. Press the ears back and flatten them out. Decorate the dog's face and tape the dog's head to a paddle pop stick.

Project 8

# Paper Bag Puppet

any size paper bag, empty toilet paper roll, newspaper, string, materials for decorating

Crumple up newspaper and stuff it into the bag. Insert the cardboard cylinder into the bag and draw up the bag around it. Tightly tie off the puppet's neck with string. Twist the corners of the bag for little ears; for larger ears, gather up a larger section of the corner and tie off with spare string. Draw a face on a separate piece of paper and paste it into the bag, or decorate the bag itself.

Project 9

# Cardboard Puppet

heavy cardboard, scissors, materials for decorating

Cut the cardboard into a rectangle about 18 cm × 10 cm. Make 2 bends near the centre of the cardboard; make the folds about 4 cm apart. (For fast, straight folding, just bend the cardboard over a table edge.) Draw a face on the puppet and maybe some teeth on the upper jaw.

Project 10

# Lolly Bag Puppet

small white lolly bags (or button bags from the haberdasher), scissors, materials for decorating

Cut a hole in both corners of the bag so the child can put a finger and a thumb through for the puppet's arms. Decorate the puppet. If you make a puppet for each hand, they can have conversations or hold hands or hug each other.

Project 11

# Envelope Puppet

small white 10 cm × 17 cm envelopes, materials for decorating

Tear the flap off an envelope. Fold the envelope in half and crease the line several times. Now open the envelope as far out as it will go without tearing. Put your fingers in the top half and thumb in the bottom half. Push the folded crease inwards. This forms the puppet's mouth. Decorate the puppet with eyes, ears, teeth, tongue, hair.

Project 12

# Running Mouse

paper, scissors, pipe cleaner, stapler, paste, black crayon

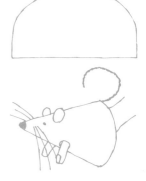

Take a piece of paper (either coloured or plain) and cut it into a rectangle approximately 20 cm long by 10 cm wide. Round off 2 corners of a long edge so you end up with a sort of semicircle. Wrap the paper into a cone large enough for the child's hand to fit into; staple. Make 2 holes in the underside of the cone so that the child's first and second fingers can poke through for the mouse's legs. Cut out and paste on 2 oval-shaped pieces of paper for the mouse's ears. Colour in eyes, a nose and some whiskers. Attach the mouse's pipe cleaner tail on the upper edge of the cone.

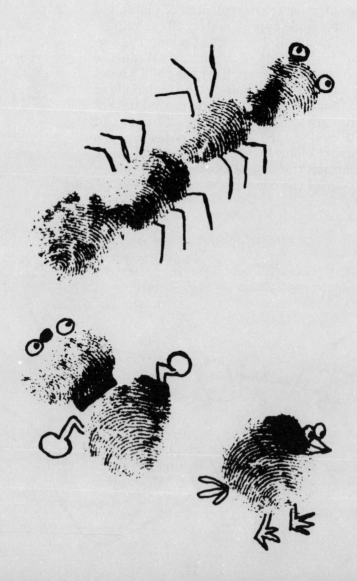

Project 13

# Fingerprint Bugs

paper, stamp pad, materials for decorating

Before beginning this project, do a few test runs on various stamp pads to see which ink washes off the fingers with the least amount of scrubbing. Let children make little fingerprint mice, bugs or just dots and lots of dots. The critters can have legs and tails drawn on. Encourage kids to try thumbs, palms and even whole hand prints. You can do this project using a shallow dish of paint, covered with a thin sponge, but the stamp pad seems to give sharper, more interesting fingerprints.

Project 14

# Carrots

background paper, orange paper, scissors, paste, green and brown crayons

Cut out some long thin orange triangles of various sizes. On the paper, draw a brown line to represent ground level. Let the children paste their carrots under the ground and then draw some green tops, above the ground. More of the earth can be coloured in, between the carrots.

Project 15

# Cotton Ball Creatures

coloured background paper, paste, cotton balls, materials for decorating

SHEEP   Draw the outline of a sheep's body onto the background paper. Let the children paste cotton balls onto the body of the sheep. Then draw on the face and legs. Or, let one cotton ball be one (small) sheep. After drawing on the legs and face, you can then finish the pastoral scene with a fence, trees, sun, cloud or whatever.

CHICKEN   Draw the outline of the chick onto the background paper. Paste down yellow cotton balls (from the packs of coloured cotton balls). Either draw on or cut out beak and legs from orange paper and paste these in place.

SNOWMAN   As for other two; paste on black hat, pipe, eyes and coat buttons.

Project 16

## Seed Coaster

Polyfilla (or some similar putty which sets hard), lid from screw top jar, dried peas, beans, seeds

Mix up the Polyfilla as directed and fill the lid with the Polyfilla. Set out a variety (in shape, colour and size) of dried beans and seeds. Let the kids push the beans into the Polyfilla; when finished, let the coaster set overnight. Very shallow lids are best for this project, as the beans cannot totally disappear below the Polyfilla and also, the coaster dries out more quickly and is less likely to develop a crack.

Project 17

## Trees

background paper, paste, leaves, crayons, dirt or sand

Using the crayon, draw a 'ground line', the tree trunk and some branches. Paste the leaves onto the tree. (This project can be even more fun if children go outdoors and collect the leaves themselves.) Spread some paste below the ground line and then sprinkle some dirt or sand onto the paper.

Project 18

# Body Outlines

large sheets of white paper, thick black Texta, materials for decorating

Explain to the children that you are going to draw their outlines and they must lie very still while you are drawing 'them'. Let the children strike a 'body pose' (one arm up and one down, hands on hips, etc.) if they want to. Using the black Texta, draw the outline of the child. When the outline is complete, let the child fill in eyes, mouth, hair and so on and then colour in some clothes. On a smaller scale (or perhaps for those who don't want to join in on the whole body outline), you can draw the outline of the child's hand or foot. Some children may want to have a turn at drawing the outlines of each other, or a doll or teddy bear. If this is the case, best change over the Texta for a thick black crayon!

Project 19

# Coloured Toothpick Pictures

coloured toothpicks, background cardboard (preferably white), paste, materials for decorating

Let children paste coloured toothpicks onto the cardboard, either in a random pattern or perhaps in a simple pattern of a star, a flower or a house. They can finish off the scene if they want with crayons or paste and paper.

Project 20

# Crumpled Creatures

crêpe paper, paste, scissors, background paper, a crayon or Texta

Cut the coloured crêpe paper into squares about 3 cm square; let the children screw the squares of paper into small balls. Draw the outline of a small sheep's body onto the background paper. Smear the body with paste and then set the crumpled balls into place. Add legs and face. Other creatures you might like to try are chickens, rabbits, flowers — just remember to keep it small.

Project 21

# Hey-There's-a Worm-on-You

thick coloured paper or lightweight cardboard, cotton balls, paste, materials for decorating, double-sided tape

Cut a strip of cardboard about 10 cm × 3 cm. Paste on a row of cotton balls for the woolly worm's body. Using any spare paper, cut out a circle for the worm's face and decorate it and paste it onto the cardboard strip; add legs, antennae or whatever. When the worm is complete, cut out two squares of double-sided tape. On the underside of the cardboard, put one piece of tape near the front end and one near the back end of the strip. Wear your worm!

## Lick-it Pictures

background paper (white or coloured), package of gummed coloured papers (the sort you just have to lick in order to make them stick), scissors

Cut out some simple geometric shapes and keep them separated from each other. The children can just choose a shape, lick it and stick it onto the background paper. Some children might want to just glue shapes on at random or you might try one of the following examples. Keep the cut pieces fairly large and simple.

CATERPILLAR   Cut out many circles from the gummed coloured paper. Children can then stick the circles down, one circle touching the next one, in any sort of pattern from a straight line to a loop-the-loop. Then just draw in some stick legs and a face.

HOUSE   Cut out a rectangle for the house, a triangle for the roof and 2 small squares for the windows on the house.

PINE TREES   3 (or more, if you want a taller tree) triangles form the trees and a small rectangle can be the trunk.

TRUCK   Large rectangle for the truck's body, 2 circles for the wheels and a square for the cabin.

Project 23

# A Most Magnificent Easter Egg

background paper or light-weight cardboard, paste, crayon, egg shells (rinsed out), yarn, glitter, coloured paper, lentils, tiny noodles

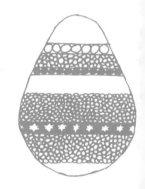

Draw the outline of a large egg onto the background paper; you can draw sections onto the egg outline and then fill each section with something different, or you can just decorate your egg however you like. Egg shells are fun to crush up, either with a hammer, rolling pin or just scrunched up in the hand. Put some paste onto a section of the egg and then sprinkle the crushed eggshell onto the paper. You can sprinkle glitter, or lentils, or tiny star-shaped noodles much the same way. Tear up scraps of coloured paper and glue them on too. Clean out the collage box! One thing's for certain —no two eggs will be alike!

Project 24

# Spaghetti Prints

spaghetti noodles, food colouring, background cardboard

Cook some spaghetti noodles in water which has had some food colouring added to it. Drain the noodles, but *do not* rinse them. Let the noodles cool down until you can touch them with your fingers. Let children lay spaghetti in patterns onto the cardboard. Leave to dry and the noodles will automatically stick to the cardboard and harden.

Project 25

# nake

paper, scissors, black paper, materials for decoration

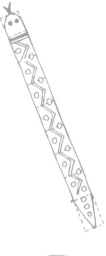

ut out a length of paper about 40 cm × 3 cm. ound off one end of the strip for the snake's head; ape the other end to a point for the tail. Cut out black eyes and a forked tongue and paste these n the snake. Decorate the body of the snake. To ish off the reptile, fold the entire length of the ake's body into an accordion fold.

Project 26

# ird

coloured paper, orange paper, scissors, paste

ut a circle of paper about 8 cm in diameter. Cut it 2 large orange triangles for the bird's beak and small triangles for the bird's tail feathers. Cut it 2 circles for the eyes and colour a black dot in e centre. For the bird's feet, cut out a rectangle orange paper so that it measures 8 cm × 4 cm. old this rectangle into thirds and cut a slot in ch short side. Paste all the parts on and stand e bird on its feet.

Project 27

# abbit

empty toilet paper roll, black paper, white paper, scissors, paste, materials for decorating

ut out a piece of white paper to cover the empty ilet roll with. Roll the white paper around the roll d tuck the ends into the cardboard cylinder. raw a face on the rabbit. Cut out two black oval- aped ears and cut a slit in the wide end of each r. Fit the ears onto the rabbit. Cut out a little ack bow tie and paste this onto the bottom of the linder.

Project 28

# Daisy

coloured paper, scissors, cotton ball, stapler, pipe cleaner, paste

Cut coloured paper into strips about 10 cm × 2 cm. Arrange these in criss-cross fashion, on top of each other. Put a staple through the centre to hold your flower together. Staple a pipe cleaner into place for the stem and finally, paste a cotton ball over the centre of the flower.

Project 29

# Plain Crêpe
# Paper Flower

crêpe paper of various colours, pipe cleaner, scissors

Cut crêpe paper into strips about 5 cm wide. Make some strips 15 cm long, some 10 cm long and some 5 cm long. Lay down a long strip, then put a medium one over the long one and then a short strip on the top. Pinch together at the middle and secure with the end of a pipe cleaner.

Project 30

# Frilly Crêpe
# Paper Flower

crêpe paper of various colours, pipe cleaner, scissors

Cut crêpe paper into strips about 5 cm wide. Lay several strips on top of each other and make several narrow parallel cuts about three-quarters of the width of the strip. Then, roll up the strips into a cylinder shape and secure with a pipe cleaner stem. Fluff out the flower's petals.

Project 31

# Giant Sunflower

paper, scissors, stapler, stick or pencil

Take a piece of paper that looks about quarto size. Fold it in half, so the fold runs across the paper. Make several parallel cuts into the fold, about 3 cm apart. Unfold the paper and roll it into a loose cylinder; staple at top and bottom. Compress the two open ends towards each other and staple at the base of the petals. Find a stem for your flower and you can also fill in the centre with wadded up paper.

Project 32

# Growing Tree

large piece of green paper (or newspaper will do), tape, scissors

Roll the paper into a tight tube. Tape around one end and also tape down the loose side. Make cuts down the tube to within about 10 cm of the taped end. Do this all the way around the tube shape. Bend down the top strips and pull upwards from the centre. Your tree will grow! (These small trees make excellent toppings for a hat too.)

# lower Pot

paper cup, scissors, cardboard, materials for decoration

ıt out a cardboard circle about the same size as
e opening of the paper cup. Put a hole in the
rdboard circle so the stem of your flower or tree
n fit through. Decorate the flower pot and plant
ur flower.

# MASKS AND CLOTHING

## pace Helmet

large brown paper bag, scissors, clear coloured cellophane, paste, materials for decorating

e paper bag is worn as a mask. Near where the ild's eyes are, cut out a rectangle about 10 cm 5 cm. Over this hole, paste a large piece of clear loured cellophane. The space helmet can be rther decorated with pipe cleaners, cupcake pers and other collage box findings.

## ox Shoes

empty tissue or cracker box or shoe box, rubber bands, materials for decorating

st the thing to wear with a space helmet! Decore the empty tissue boxes (1 for each foot) and ear them over normal shoes. Or, use the bottom lf of shoe boxes (upside-down) and cut a hole st large enough to slip a foot through. Small feet large holes may need a rubber band around the x to hold the shoe in place. Great for clomping out.

Project 36

# Paper Plate Cat Mask

paper plate (15 cm wide ones for small children), lightweight cardboard or coloured paper, drinking straws, stapler, scissors, paddle pop stick or tongue depressor, crayons

Cut out triangular-shaped cardboard ears and staple them in place. For the cat's whiskers, criss-cross 3 drinking straws and secure them onto the mask with a staple. Cut out eye holes and mouth hole and draw in eyelashes and eyebrows. Staple the mask to a tongue depressor. This is a good mask for very young children, as it can come 'on' and 'off' with a minimum of fuss.

Project 37

# Paper Bag Clothing

large brown paper bag, scissors, string, materials for decorating

There are any number of garments you can make from an ordinary grocery bag.

SMOCK TOP    Cut a hole in the bottom of the bag for the child's head and then 2 smaller holes in the narrow sides of the bag for the armholes.

WALKING SHORTS    Cut 2 holes in the bottom corners of the bag for the child's legs. So the shorts will stay up easily, tie a piece of string around the waist.

SKIRT    Cut a hole in the bottom of the bag; this hole will go around the child's waist. Around the large hole, punch a number of small holes and lace a piece of string around the hole. Tighten and tie with a bow—this should keep the skirt in place.

Project 38

# Paper Plate Rabbit Mask

paper plate, scissors, stapler, string or hat elastic, materials for decorating

Cut away a wedge-shaped piece, equal to about a fifth of the circle. Overlap the cut edges and staple to form a flat cone-shaped mask. Staple on 2 oval-shaped ears. Cut out eye holes and mouth hole. Decorate the mask further and attach strings or hat elastic to hold the mask in place.

Project 39

# Embroidered Vest

mesh from large bags used for fruit and vegetables, scissors, yarn, tape

Cut out a vest from the bag. Cut a hole in the bottom of the bag for the neck, an opening down the front of the vest and 2 armholes. Cut yarn into manageable lengths. Wind tape around one end of a length of yarn to form a 'needle' for sewing. Let children thread the yarn through the mesh of their vests.

Project 40

# Beards

cardboard or heavy paper, scissors, crêpe paper, cotton balls, paste, hat elastic

Cut out a 15 cm wide semi-circle of cardboard or heavy paper. Cut out a mouth hole. Either paste cotton balls onto white cardboard for a white beard, or, paste strips of black crêpe paper onto black coloured cardboard (for a black beard). Punch 2 holes in the sides of the beard and tie the hat elastic through so the beard will stay up.

# EGG CARTON CRAFT

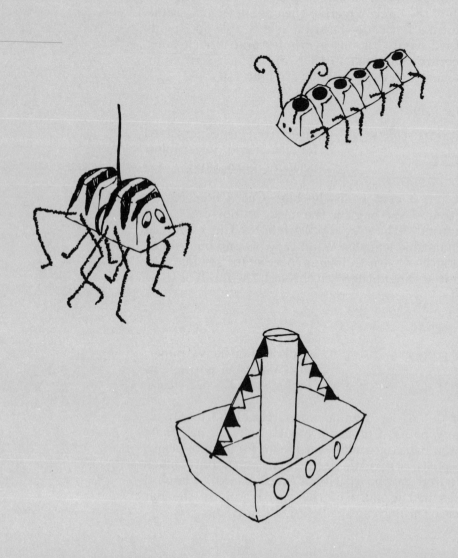

## Project 41

# Tiger Claws

egg carton, scissors, yellow and black coloured paper, paste, rubber bands

Take one egg carton and cut it in half. Cut jagged 'claws' into the front and side edges of the lids. Cut the coloured paper into 'tiger stripes' about 10 cm x 2 cm. Paste the tiger stripes onto the top of the egg carton claws. Put a rubber band around the egg carton near the last claw; this should hold the claws on. Much roaring and snarling follows.

## Project 42

# Egg Carton Face

egg carton, coloured paper, paste, scissors, crayon

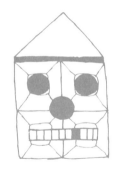

Cut the bottom section of an egg carton so that you have four adjoining egg cups. From the coloured paper, cut out a triangular shaped hat and paste this to the top of the carton. Cut out two small circles and paste these in the bottoms of two adjoining egg cups. Cut out a larger circle for the nose and paste this circle in the high centre section. Cut out a long, narrow rectangular strip and mark some teeth on it with a crayon. Paste this in the bottom two egg cups and across the ridge.

## Project 43

# Egg Carton Octopus

egg carton, scissors, pipe cleaners, materials for decorating

Take one egg cup from the bottom of an egg carton and cut a U-shape into each of the four sides. Poke holes in the four bottom corners. Into each of the holes, insert a pipe cleaner to about half its length. Twist the pipe cleaner several times to make the octopus's tentacles.

Project 44

# Egg Carton Umbrella

egg carton, piece of dowel stick, paper, paste, scissors, materials for decorating

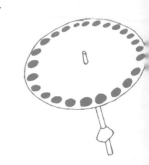

Cut out a circle of paper about 20 cm in diameter. This is the top of the umbrella; decorate it. Paste the centre of the circle onto an end of the dowel. Take a single egg cup from an egg carton and punch a hole in the bottom of it. Slip the egg cup, upside-down, onto the dowel stick. Children can then slide the egg cup up and down the stick, and though their umbrellas are always open, they don't seem to mind.

Project 45

# Egg Carton Boat

egg carton, empty toilet paper roll, paste, tape, materials for decorating, string, coloured paper

Take the lid from an egg carton and cut it in half. Tape the empty toilet roll in the centre of the boat so that it forms a smokestack. Punch a small hole in the front of the boat and tie on a piece of string. Take the string over the top of the smokestack and then tie the string to a small hole punched in the back of the boat. Cut out some small diamond-shaped pieces of coloured paper. Put a bit of paste onto each half of the diamond shape and then fold it around the string. This makes little flags along the string. Decorate the boat further if you want with waves, portholes and a name.

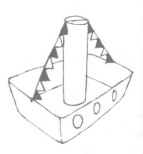

# Egg Carton Caterpillar

egg carton, scissors, pipe cleaners, materials for decorating

Make a caterpillar from a length of six adjoining egg cups. Decorate the first cup with pipe cleaner antennae and a face. You can also poke some holes in the egg cups and attach pipe cleaner legs (if you have enough pipe cleaners).

Project 47

# Egg Carton Spider

egg carton, pipe cleaners, yarn or string, materials for decorating

Take two adjoining egg cups from an egg carton; this is the body. Attach pipe cleaner legs — as many as you like! Decorate your spider with crayons, Textas or coloured paper and paste. To finish off the project, cut a length of yarn or string about ½ m long. Tie one end to the spider's body. The spider can then be dangled along the floor.

Project 48

# Egg Carton Bumble Bee

egg carton, coloured paper, scissors, paste, pipe cleaner, materials for decorating

Take two adjoining cups for the bee's body. Cut out two triangular-shaped wings and paste these onto the body. Make two antennae for the bee and decorate the bee with crayons or paste and paper.

# TOYS AND GAMES

roject 49

# aper Cup

heavy white paper, scissors, materials for decorating

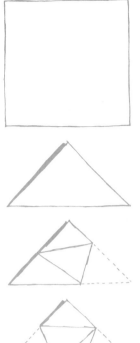

ut paper into a 15 cm square. Fold the paper into triangle. Take one base corner of the triangle and old it over so that the point touches the middle of he opposite side. Do the same with the other base orner, folding it towards its opposite side. You hould now have two small triangular pieces at the op of your cup. Fold one triangle over the back nd one over the front. Decorate the cup and then op it open—just the thing for a serving of ultanas.

Project 50

# Pinwheel

paper, new unsharpened pencil with an eraser on the end, scissors, straight pin, materials for decorating

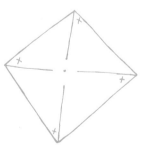

Cut the paper into a 15 cm square. It's easiest to decorate the pinwheel now. From each corner of the square, make a diagonal cut towards the centre. Stop cutting about 3 cm from the centre. Bring the right half of each of the four corners to the centre. When the four corners are gathered this way, put a straight pin through the place where all the papers meet. Push the straight pin into, but not completely through, the pencil eraser. Blow.

Project 51

# Helicopter

paper, scissors, tape, crayons

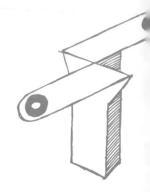

Trace the pattern shown in the illustration onto plain paper. Cut on the solid lines and fold on the dotted lines. Fold back the two bottom sections to form a sort of handle. (For the best aerodynamics, tape these pieces so they stay firmly back.) Fold one of the two top sections forward and one back. The helicopter works best if dropped, either by a tall adult or perhaps from the veranda steps. The helicopter should twirl its way to earth. Children can personalise their helicopters with crayons or coloured pencils, but avoid pasting on any decorations, as with the added paper weight, the rotor blades do not respond as well as they should.

Project 52

# The Green Haired Creature

egg shell, dirt, Textas, cress seeds

The empty egg shell from a boiled breakfast egg is perfect. Clean out shell and decorate with a face. Fill the shell with dirt and sprinkle some cress seeds (or grass seeds will do) on top. Moisten the dirt. After a couple of days you can give the creature a hair cut and put the cress on a sandwich or in scrambled eggs.

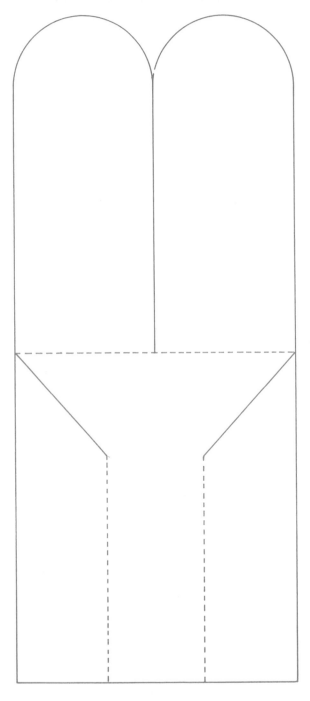

Project 53

# Boomerangs

thin cardboard, scissors, crayons

Copy any of the four designs onto thin cardboard and then cut out. Decorate the boomerang with crayons. There are two methods of flying the boomerangs. The first is easier for younger children; the second takes a bit more co-ordination, but often the boomerang flys better. *Method 1:* Rest the boomerang on the back of one hand. Use the pointer finger of the other hand to flick the extended leg of the boomerang. *Method 2:* Very lightly, hold the middle of the boomerang between the thumb and pointer finger. Have the two ends pointing towards you. Use the pointer finger of the other hand to sharply strike one of the legs.

Project 54

# Tambourine

foil plate, string, foil milk caps, scissors

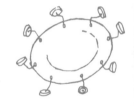

Make holes around the edges of a foil plate, either by snipping holes with the scissors, or by punching holes in the plate with the ends of the scissors (or some other instrument such as a ball-point pen). Punch a hole in a milk bottle lid and tie the lid to the plate with a length of string about 8 cm long. Do this all around the edge of the plate.

Project 55

# Edible Jewellery

string, scissors, cereal or snack food with a hole in it

Cut a length of string that will serve as a bracelet or necklace. String the cereal or snack food onto the necklace. When complete, tie off and wear the jewellery for a while—then eat it!

Project 56

# Binoculars

empty toilet rolls, stapler, clear coloured cellophane, tape, string

Staple two empty toilet rolls together. Cut two circles of coloured cellophane about the same size as the open end of the toilet roll tubes; tape the cellophane over the ends of the tubes. Attach a string neckstrap to the binoculars and then go outside and look around.

Project 57

# Echidna

small potatoes, coloured paper, paste, used match-sticks or toothpicks

Using the matchsticks, fit a couple of small potatoes together. Cover the head and body of the echidna with used matches or toothpicks. Cut out some eyes, ears and a mouth from the coloured paper, and paste (or pin) these onto the potatoes.

Project 58

# Basket

lightweight cardboard, scissors, stapler, materials for decorating

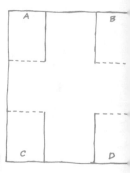

Cut out a rectangle of cardboard about 25 cm × 20 cm. Cut four slots as shown in the illustration; fold along the dotted lines. Overlap sections A and B and then staple these two together. Do the same at the other end with C and D sections. Pull up the remaining flap and staple this one in place too. Cut out a handle from cardboard and staple this onto the two thick ends. Decorate the basket.

# Gone Fishing

paper, string, scissors, paper clip, tape, stick (or strong plastic drinking straw), materials for decorating

Cut out a 15 cm square of paper and put a dot in the centre. Fold all the corners to the centre. Open out two adjoining corners and cut slits from the corner to the fold line. From this point onwards, you can make two different sorts of fish. For the *finned fish*, fold the two inner wedges to the centre; the outside wedges are the fins. For the *tailed fish*, fold the two outside wedges to the centre so that the other two wedges become the tail. Tape down all the flaps. Decorate the fish. Tie a length of string to the stick and tie a paper clip to the end of string. Children can then catch a fish by slipping the nose of the fish onto the paper clip.

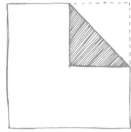

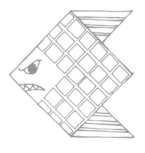

Project 60

# Kazoo

empty toilet roll, scissors, greaseproof paper, rubber band, materials for decorating

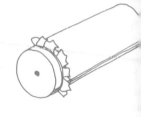

Cut out a square of greaseproof paper and fit this over one end of an empty toilet roll; secure with a rubber band. Using a pencil or ball-point pen, poke a hole in the middle of the greaseproof paper. Hold the open end of the kazoo close around your lips and sing or yell. *Note:* some youngsters blow or make sounds which do not vibrate well. One of the best noises to start off with is 'whoo whoo' like a train. This usually gives a good kazoo noise.

Project 61

# Lantern

paper, scissors, stapler

Fold the paper in half and make some parallel cuts into the fold. Unfold paper and roll it into a loose cylinder. Staple at the top and bottom. Cut out a thin paper handle and staple this into place.

Project 62

# Leaping Frogs

very thin Y-shaped twig from a tree, or wishbone from a turkey or chicken, small straight twig, rubber band

Hunting for the materials for this project is almost as much fun as making it—what a good excuse for a walk. Stretch the rubber band across the two ends of the Y-shaped stick. Put the straight piece of stick through the rubber band and wind the straight stick around and around. Put your leaping frog onto the floor and suddenly take your hands away.

# Paper Chain

paper, stapler, scissors

Cut paper into strips about 20 cm × 2½ cm. To begin the paper chain, overlap the two ends of one paper strip and staple. This makes a circle. Take the next strip, fit it through the circle and then staple its ends together. A paper chain can be a necklace, a party decoration, or it can be taped to a stick for an interesting flag to wave around.

Project 64

# Wriggling Spider

lightweight cardboard, rubber bands, scissors, tape, string, a stick, materials for decorating

Trace the spider shape onto the cardboard and cut out. Decorate the spider. Cut a 40 cm length of string. Poke a hole in the centre of the spider and push the string through the hole; tape string to the underside of the spider's body. Bend the head down, along the dotted line. Cut some rubber bands in half and tape them to the underside of the spider. Tie the free end of the string to a stick and see whom you can scare!

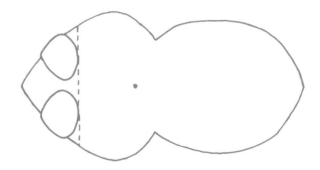

47

## Project 65
# Egg Face

egg shell, paper, scissors, stapler, Textas

Clean out a half egg shell and decorate it with a face. Make a hat by cutting out a circle of paper, removing a wedge from the circle, overlap the edges and staple them. Cut out another circle of paper about 10 cm in diameter. Cut a slit that reaches to the centre and cut away a circle of paper from the centre, so you end up with a doughnut shape. Overlap the edges quite a bit and staple. This will make a little stand for egg face to sit on. Egg face is a good place for little treasures!

## Project 66
# Matchbox Boat

empty matchbox, toothpick, small piece of stiff white paper, straight pin

Cut out some sail shapes in the white paper—either triangles or squares about 4–6 cm wide work fine. Poke a small hole in the matchbox and two holes in the sail. Insert the toothpick mast into the sail and then onto the boat. These boats sail well in a tub of water or in the bath.

## Project 67
# Non-Flying Kite

paper sandwich bags, stapler, string, crêpe paper, scissors, materials for decorating

Staple the crêpe paper tail to a corner of the sandwich bag. Make a few twists in the tail. Decorate the kite with paste and paper or maybe crayons or Textas. Tie the string onto the corner opposite the tail. These kites won't really fly, but children love to drag them along while running.

Project 68

# Sweet Smeller

small apple or lemon, toothpick, whole cloves, cinnamon, square of loose-weave material, ribbon

Using the toothpick, poke a hole into the fruit. Stuff a whole clove into the hole. Cover the entire fruit in the same way. Set fruit onto the square of material and sprinkle with cinnamon. Draw up cloth and tie with ribbon. Leave sweet smeller undisturbed for a while; ball will smell its best after it has dried out a little. A good gift for anybody's wardrobe. *Note:* If the smell should weaken after a while, just sprinkle sweet smeller with a little water.

Project 69

# Spinning Top

cardboard, scissors, pencil (either new or used), materials for decorating

Cut out a circle of cardboard about 9 cm in diameter. Decorate the top side of the cardboard— spirals or pie-shaped segments make interesting patterns when the top spins. Poke a hole in the centre of the circle and fit the pencil into the hole so that it fits snugly. The pencil should be about 15 cm long; insert the pencil so that about 3 cm sticks through. The eraser end is fine for spinning.

## Project 70

# Glider

paper, scissors, paper clip, materials for decorating

Cut paper into a 15 cm square. Fold paper in half and trace glider pattern onto the paper. Cut the glider out, but don't cut along the folded edge. Now is a good time to do the decorating. Fold down the tail and wings. Put a paper clip onto the nose of the glider to give it a bit of weight. Fly away.

## Project 71

# Curly Basket

paper cup, scissors, pipe cleaner, pencil, materials for decorating

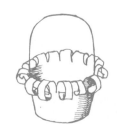

Fringe the edge of a paper cup by making parallel cuts down to about 3 cm or 4 cm from the bottom. Curl the edges either by rolling the paper up with your fingers or by rolling the paper around a pencil. Attach a pipe cleaner handle.

## Project 72

# Rattler

paper plates, dried beans or pebbles, stapler, tongue depressor, tape, materials for decorating

Decorate the underneath side of two paper plates. Hold the plates face-to-face, place the beans in between the plates and staple the two plates together, using several staples around the edge of the plates. Partially insert a tongue depressor into the rattle and then tape it firmly in place.

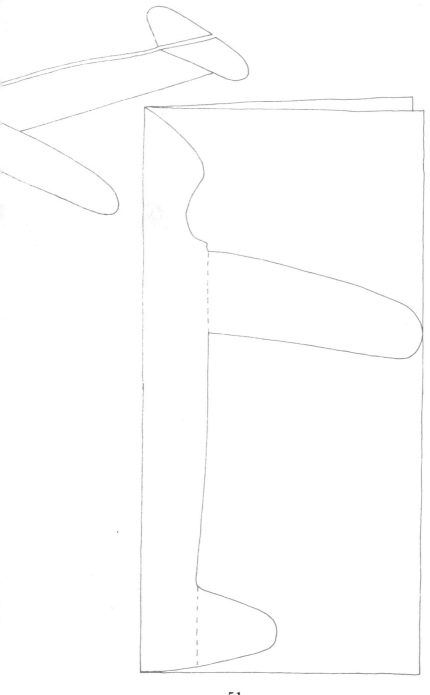

Project 73

# Sports Car

cardboard box large enough for a child to sit in, scissors, materials for decorating

To make things easier for the craft organiser, everyone should supply a cardboard box on the day your group decides to do this project. Make a backwards L-shaped cut in the side of the box for the car door. Spend the rest of the time decorating and driving the sports cars. Some suggestions for decorating: red Texta tail lights; small pie plates for headlights, or just some small circles cut and pasted into place; front and back licence plates; speedometer, buttons and switches drawn on the cardboard; petrol cap; wheels; if the box has a front flap, cut a rectangle in it for a windscreen.

Project 74

# Woolly Worms

cardboard, tape, scissors, crayons or Textas, very thick craft yarn, double-sided tape

Cut out a circle of cardboard about 3 cm in diameter. Draw a face on the cardboard with crayons or Textas. Cut a length of craft yarn about 15 cm or so long. Tape the yarn onto the back of the cardboard circle. Children might like to wear their woolly worms. Put a small square of double-sided tape onto the back of the worm face and then stick the worm onto the child's shirt.

Project 75

# Paper Whistle   lightweight paper, scissors

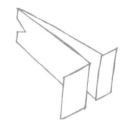

Cut a strip of paper about 12 cm × 3 cm (actually, the whistle can be almost any dimension, but this size seems a good one for young children to manage). Fold it in half lengthwise. Fold back the ends about 1·5 cm. Cut a notch in the centre of the folded end. Hold the folded-back ends loosely near the lips and blow. The paper will vibrate and make a sort of whistling noise. Send the children outside to play after *this* craft project is over!

Project 76

# Flags

rectangles of cloth material (preferably white or some light colour), stapler, dowel stick or some other thin wood, materials for decorating

Decorate the flag material with paints, crayons, Textas. Roll one side of the flag at least once around the dowel stick and staple the cloth several times. Encourage children to stand well away from each other when flag waving.

Project 77

# Fuzzy Ball   cardboard, yarn, scissors

For each fuzzy ball, cut out two circles of cardboard 8 cm in diameter. Cut a 1·5 cm hole in the centre of each cardboard circle, so you end up with two doughnut shapes. Hold the two circles together. Use a little ball of yarn that will pass through the centre hole easily. Start by holding the end of the yarn on the outer edge of the cardboard (it's best to tape this end temporarily onto the cardboard). Push the ball of wool through the centre hole and then around the outer edge. Work your way around the circle of cardboard. Cut the yarn around the edge of the cardboard. Separate the cardboard a little and tie a piece of yarn around the centre, between the two pieces of cardboard. Then, slip the cardboard circles off.

Project 78

# Purse   paper, stapler, scissors, yarn or string, materials for decorating

Cut the paper to about quarto size. Fold it into three, with one end smaller than the other two folds (this is the flap). Staple along the sides of the purse, but be sure not to staple the flap down. Tie on a length of yarn or string, so the purse can be worn over the shoulder or around the waist. Decorate the purse. Provide a few items for children to put in their purses—milk bottle caps, old keys, ticket stubs, a tissue, pencil and paper.

Project 79

# Jack-in-the-Matchbox

empty matchbox, paper, paste, scissors, materials for decorating

Cut a strip of paper about 6 cm × 2 cm; cut out a circle of paper 2 cm in diameter. Draw a little face on the circle of paper and paste the circle onto one end of the paper strip. Fold the strip of paper, back and forth, accordion-fashion. Paste the free end of the strip inside the matchbox. Squash the jack-in-the-matchbox down into the matchbox and slide the lid on. Then, quickly open the box.

Project 80

# Paddle Boat

wood, hammer, nails, wide rubber band

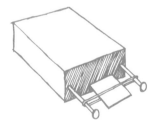

Any scrap of wood about 5 cm × 10 cm will do. Hammer two long nails into one end of the block; only hammer them in just far enough so they don't fall out. Keep the nails as far apart as you can. Use a wide rubber band that's about as big as the distance between the two nails (or, you can use a narrow rubber band and double it over). Stretch the rubber band between the two nails, near the end. Find a thin, flat scrap of wood for the paddle. Insert the paddle between the nails, centre it and wind it up. Take your paddle boat to a tub of water for its launching.

Project 81

# Spinner

cardboard, scissors, string, materials for decorating

Cut out a cardboard circle about 7 cm in diameter. Cut out some teeth edges if you like and decorate the spinner. Mark the centre of the spinner with a small dot. Make two small holes 3 mm on each side of the centre dot. Cut two V-shaped notches with the scissors. Thread the string through the holes and tie the two loose ends together. Hold a loop in each hand. Twist the disc to wind up the string (or have a helpful friend wind up the string for you). Pull the string to get the spinner going. Get a pull-apart—come-together—pull-apart—come-together motion going.

For days when everyone wants a change from craft activities . . . try these edible projects!

Project 82

# No Cook Cereal Balls

½ C chunky peanut butter
⅓ C honey
½ C coconut
2 C favourite cereal

Put peanut butter, honey, coconut into a bowl and mix well. Stir in ½ C of the cereal and put the rest of the cereal into a bowl. Scoop out spoonfuls of the peanut butter mixture and form into balls with your hands. Roll the balls in the large bowl of cereal until covered (the balls, not you).

# No Bake Party Cakes

packet of plain, flat, sweet biscuits (Milk Arrowroot, etc)
bowl of icing
bowl of hundreds and thousands
spreaders (paddle pop sticks, plastic knives, etc)

Let each child spread a biscuit with icing and then dip the biscuit into the bowl of hundreds and thousands (and yes, there will be individuals who will ignore the biscuits and just eat the icing—and vice versa!).

# MATERIALS LIST

Below are listed the main materials needed for each project. Often substitutions can be made, so be sure to refer to the detailed instructions before you pass over a project due to lack of an item. The materials for decorating' have been left off this listing.

*paper, scissors* Paper Cup, Paper Whistle
*paper, stamp pad* Fingerprint Bugs
*paper, tape* Sailor Hat
*paper, scissors, stapler* Dutch Hat, Sun Hat, Skull Cap, Lantern, Paper Chain
*paper, scissors, tape* Growing Tree, Helicopter
*paper, scissors, gummed coloured paper* Lick-It Pictures
*paper, scissors, black paper* Snake
*paper, scissors, paper clip* Glider
*paper, scissors, orange paper, paste, crayon* Carrots, Bird
*paper, scissors, tape, paddle pop stick* Dog on a Stick
*paper, scissors, tape, string, paper clip, stick* Gone Fishing
*paper, scissors, stapler, string* Purse
*paper, scissors, stapler, pipe cleaner* Indian Headband
*paper, scissors, stapler, pipe cleaner, paste* Running Mouse
*paper, scissors, stapler, pencil* Paper Crown, Giant Sunflower
*paper, scissors, stapler, pipe cleaner, cotton ball* Daisy
*paper, scissors, new pencil with eraser, straight pin* Pinwheel
*paper, paste, leaves, crayons* Trees
*paper, paste, crayon, egg shells, yarn, glitter, lentils, noodles* A Most Magnificent Easter Egg
*large sheet of white paper, black Texta* Body Outlines

*crêpe paper, plain paper, paste, crayons* Crumpled Creatures

*crêpe paper, scissors, pipe cleaner* Plain Crêpe Paper Flower, Frilly Crêpe Paper Flower

*paper plate, stapler, dried beans or rocks* Rattler

*paper plate, scissors, stapler, string* Paper Plate Rabbit Mask

*paper plate, cardboard, drinking straws, stapler, scissors, tongue depressor* Paper Plate Cat Mask

*paper cup, cardboard, scissors* Flower Pot

*paper cup, scissors, pipe cleaner* Curly Basket

*paper sandwich bag, scissors, stapler, string, crêpe paper* Non-Flying Kite

*paper bag, empty toilet paper roll, newspaper, string* Paper Bag Puppet

*small white lolly bag, scissors* Lolly Bag Puppet

*large shopping bag, scissors, clear coloured cellophane, paste* Space Helmet

*large shopping bag, scissors, string* Paper Bag Clothing

*small envelope* Envelope Puppet

*cardboard, scissors, string* Spinner

*cardboard, scissors, pencil* Spinning Top

*cardboard, scissors, tape, thick craft yarn, Textas, double-sided tape* Woolly Worm

*lightweight cardboard, scissors, paste, cotton balls or black crêpe paper, hat elastic* Beards

*lightweight cardboard, cotton balls, paste, double-sided tape.* Hey-There's-a-Worm-on-You

*lightweight cardboard, rubber bands, scissors, tape, string, a stick* Wriggling Spider

*lightweight cardboard, scissors* Boomerangs

*lightweight cardboard, scissors, stapler* Basket

*heavy cardboard, scissors* Cardboard Puppet

*coloured paper, paste, cotton balls* Cotton Ball Sheep, Chicken, Snowman

*egg carton, scissors, yellow and black coloured paper, paste, rubber bands* Tiger Claws gg carton, scissors, coloured paper, paste Egg Carton Face

gg carton, scissors, coloured paper, paste, pipe cleaner Egg Carton Bumble Bee

gg carton, scissors, pipe cleaner Egg Carton Octopus, Caterpillar

gg carton, scissors, pipe cleaner, string Egg Carton Spider

gg carton, scissors, pipe cleaner, string Egg Carton Spider

gg carton, empty toilet paper roll, coloured paper, string, paste, tape Egg Carton Boat

gg carton, dowel stick, scissors, paper, paste Egg Carton Umbrella

npty toilet paper roll, greaseproof paper, scissors, rubber band Kazoo

npty toilet paper roll, scissors, paste, black paper, white paper Rabbit

npty toilet paper roll, stapler, clear coloured cellophane, tape, string Binoculars

gg shell, dirt, cress seeds, Textas The Green Haired Creature

gg shell, paper, scissors, stapler, Textas Egg Face

real or snack food with a hole in it, string, scissors Edible Jewellery

nall raw potato, used matchsticks or toothpicks, coloured paper, paste Echidna

ople or lemon, whole cloves, toothpicks, cinnamon, square of loose-weave cloth material Sweet Smeller

eanut butter, honey, coconut, cereal No Cook Cereal Balls

lain biscuits, icing, hundreds and thousands, paddle pop sticks No Bake Party Cakes

ood, hammer, nails, wide rubber band Paddle Boat

in Y-shaped stick, small straight stick, rubber band Leaping Frogs

npty matchbox, paper, paste, scissors Jack-in-the-Matchbox

61

*empty matchbox, toothpick, stiff white paper*
Matchbox Boat
*Polyfilla, lid from screw top jar, dried peas, beans,*
*seeds* Seed Coaster
*coloured toothpicks, cardboard, paste* Coloured
Toothpick Pictures
*empty tissue box or cracker box, rubber bands*
Box Shoes
*large cardboard box, scissors* Sports Car
*mesh from large bags of fruit and vegetables,*
*scissors, yarn, tape* Embroidered Vest
*foil plate, string, foil milk caps, scissors* Tam-
bourine
*yarn, cardboard, scissors* Fuzzy Ball
*cloth, stapler, stick* Flag
*spaghetti noodles, food colouring, cardboard*
Spaghetti Prints

# PROJECTS INDEX

# What Can I Be?

## Written by Cari Meister
## Illustrated by Matt Phillips

## SCHOLASTIC INC.

New York  Toronto  London  Auckland  Sydney
Mexico City  New Delhi  Hong Kong  Buenos Aires

**For Simon and Corrina**
—C.M.

**To Mrs. Phillips, the best teacher
in the whole world**
—M.P.

Reading Consultants

**Linda Cornwell**
Literacy Specialist

**Katharine A. Kane**
Education Consultant
(Retired, San Diego County Office of Education
and San Diego State University)

ISBN 0-516-24470-1

12 11 10 9 8 7 6 5          3 4 5 6 7 8/0

Printed in the U.S.A.                    61

First Scholastic printing, September 2003